Report to Congressional Requesters

I0412768

June 2000

AVIATION SECURITY

Long-Standing Problems Impair Airport Screeners' Performance

GAO

Accountability * Integrity * Reliability

Contents

Figures

Abbreviations

DOT   Department of Transportation
FAA   Federal Aviation Administration
GAO   General Accounting Office

G A O

Accountability * Integrity * Reliability

United States General Accounting Office
Washington, D.C. 20548

Resources, Community, and
Economic Development Division

B-282286

June 28, 2000

The Honorable John McCain
Chairman
The Honorable Ernest Hollings
Ranking Minority Member
Committee on Commerce, Science,
 and Transportation
United States Senate

The Honorable Slade Gorton
Chairman
The Honorable John D. Rockefeller IV
Ranking Minority Member
Subcommittee on Aviation
Committee on Commerce, Science,
 and Transportation
United States Senate

This report responds to your request that we study the performance of screeners at our nation's airports. The report includes recommendations to better implement the management and evaluation of FAA's efforts to improve screeners' performance.

Unless you publicly announce its contents earlier, we plan no further distribution of this report until 15 days after the date of this letter. At that time, we will send copies to the appropriate congressional committees; the Honorable Rodney E. Slater, Secretary of Transportation; the Honorable Jane F. Garvey, Administrator, Federal Aviation Administration; the Honorable Jacob J. Lew, Director, Office of Management and Budget; and other interested parties. We will make copies available to others upon request.

If you or your staff have any questions, please call me or John Schulze, Assistant Director, at (202) 512-2834. Key contributors to this report are listed in appendix I.

Gerald L. Dillingham, Ph.D.
Associate Director, Transportation Issues

Executive Summary

Purpose

The threat of attacks on aircraft by terrorists or others remains a persistent and growing concern for the United States. According to the Federal Bureau of Investigation, the trend in terrorism against U.S. targets is toward large-scale incidents designed for maximum destruction, terror, and media impact—exactly what terrorists intended in a 1995 plot to blow up 12 U.S. airliners in a single day. That plot, uncovered by police in the Philippines, focused on U.S. airliners operating in the Pacific region, but concerns are growing about the potential for attacks within the United States.

The United States and other countries have a number of safeguards in place to prevent attacks against commercial aircraft. Among the most important of these are the checkpoints at airports where passengers and their carry-on items are screened for dangerous objects, such as guns, and explosives. Historically, however, screeners who operate checkpoints in the United States have had difficulty in detecting dangerous objects, missing as many as 20 percent during tests, and numerous reports, including two by presidential commissions, have detailed significant problems with screeners' performance. Concerned about the effectiveness of screening checkpoints and of the efforts to improve them, the Senate Committee on Commerce, Science, and Transportation and its Subcommittee on Aviation requested that GAO examine (1) the causes of screeners' problems in detecting dangerous objects and the efforts of the Federal Aviation Administration (FAA) to address these problems and (2) the screening practices of selected foreign countries and the potential for using these practices to help improve screeners' performance in the United States.

Background

FAA is responsible for overseeing the safety and security of the nation's civil aviation system. Since 1973, after a spate of hijackings, the agency has required that air carriers maintain screening checkpoints to prevent or deter passengers from carrying dangerous objects aboard aircraft. While the airlines are responsible for screening activities, they generally contract with security companies to manage the checkpoints and to provide screeners, who check over 2 million passengers and their carry-on items each day. The screeners scan individuals for weapons or other dangerous objects by using metal detectors, and they examine carry-on baggage using X-ray machines, explosive detection equipment, and physical searches.

As part of its regulatory oversight of the screening operations, FAA tests screeners' ability to locate test objects placed in carry-on baggage or hidden on an FAA agent's person. The agents use standard test objects, such as guns, during these compliance tests, and FAA can fine an airline if an object is missed. FAA also tests screeners using more sophisticated simulated bombs—called improvised explosive devices—that are more difficult to detect; however, FAA views these tests as a training tool and does not issue fines when screeners miss the test objects. Concerns have long existed over screeners' performance in these tests. In 1978, screeners failed to detect 13 percent of the objects during compliance tests, and in 1987, screeners were missing 20 percent of the objects during the same type of test. Since 1997, FAA has designated data on test results as sensitive security information. Consequently, more recent data on test results cannot be released publicly and are discussed in a separate, limited-distribution report.[1] Nevertheless, FAA acknowledges that screeners' performance in detecting dangerous objects during its testing is not satisfactory.

Aviation terrorism is a concern not only in the United States but also in other countries, some of which have had more attacks than the United States, and virtually all countries conduct preboard screening operations before allowing passengers to board aircraft. Each country can—and often does—conduct screening operations in a manner that differs from that of the United States or of other countries.

Results in Brief

Long-standing problems combine to reduce screeners' effectiveness in detecting dangerous objects, most notably (1) the rapid turnover of screener personnel—often above 100 percent a year at large airports and, in at least one recent instance, above 400 percent a year and (2) human factors conditions that have for years affected screeners' hiring, training, and working environment. A key factor in the rapid turnover is the low wages screeners receive. Screeners are often paid the minimum wage or close to it and can often earn more at airport fast-food restaurants. FAA is pursuing several initiatives to improve the hiring, training, and testing of screeners; to increase their alertness and more closely monitor their performance; and to certify the security companies that air carriers retain to staff screening checkpoints; however, most of these efforts are behind schedule. Furthermore, FAA has established performance improvement goals for screeners, but it has not (1) completed an integrated plan to tie its

---

[1] *Aviation Security: Screeners Continue to Have Difficulty Detecting Dangerous Objects* (GAO/RCED-00-159, June 2000).

various efforts to improve screeners' performance to the achievement of its goals and (2) adequately measured its progress in achieving its goals for improving screeners' performance. This report contains recommendations to better implement the management and evaluation of FAA's efforts to improve screeners' performance.

Passenger screening procedures in the countries GAO visited are similar to those in the United States. Passengers walk through metal detectors at airport checkpoints and have their carry-on baggage scanned by X-ray machines or physically searched by screeners. But there are also some differences: For example, in most countries, screeners must undergo more extensive training; screeners receive higher wages and better benefits; and screening responsibility rests with the government or the airport, not with the air carriers as it does in the United States. Among the five countries GAO visited—Belgium, Canada, France, the Netherlands, and the United Kingdom—the turnover rate for screeners was lower—about 50 percent a year or less—and in a joint test conducted by FAA and one of these countries, screeners' performance was higher. However, the feasibility of applying these countries' practices to screening operations in the United States cannot be readily determined. Given this uncertainty and the fact that FAA has already begun several efforts to improve screeners' performance, GAO is not making recommendations to revise current screening practices in the United States.

GAO provided a draft of this report to the Department of Transportation for its review and comment. GAO met with FAA officials, who were responding for the Department of Transportation. These officials generally agreed with the facts presented in the draft report and acknowledged that screeners' performance needs to improve. The officials agreed with the recommendation to promptly complete the agency's integrated checkpoint screening management plan. However, they disagreed with the need to revise FAA's goal for reporting improvements in screeners' performance under the Government Performance and Results Act. GAO continues to believe that its recommendation is appropriate and consequently did not revise it. FAA officials also provided technical clarifications, which were incorporated in the report as appropriate.

Long-Standing Problems and Program Delays Impair Improvements in Screeners' Performance

Long-standing problems with screeners' performance are attributable to a number of causes. Foremost among these is the rapid turnover of screeners. Because turnover occurs so often, few experienced screeners staff the checkpoints. From May 1998 through April 1999, turnover among screeners at 19 large airports averaged over 125 percent, and one airport reported turnover of over 400 percent. According to FAA and the aviation industry, this turnover is largely due to the low pay and few, if any, benefits screeners receive, as well as the daily stress of the job. It is not unusual for the starting wages at airport fast-food restaurants to be higher than the wages screeners receive. For instance, at one airport GAO visited, screeners' wages started as low as $6.25 an hour, whereas the starting wage at one of the airport's fast-food restaurants was $7 an hour.

The human factors associated with screening—those work-related issues that are influenced by human capabilities and constraints—have also been noted by FAA as problems affecting performance for over 20 years. Screening duties require repetitive tasks as well as intense monitoring for the very rare moment when a dangerous object may be observed. Too little attention has been given to factors such as (1) individuals' aptitudes for effectively performing screening duties, (2) the sufficiency of the training provided to screeners and how well they comprehend it, and (3) the monotony of the job and the distractions that reduce screeners' vigilance. As a result, screeners are being placed on the job without having the abilities or knowledge required to perform the work effectively. Such screeners then find their duties tedious and unstimulating.

FAA has several initiatives under way to address these problems and improve screeners' performance. These include

- improving the hiring and preparation of screeners through selection tests, computer-based training, and competency tests;
- a system to keep screeners alert and monitor their performance by periodically projecting images of dangerous objects onto the monitors of the X-ray machines at checkpoints and recording the screeners' responses; and
- a certification program to make screening companies, along with the air carriers, accountable for the training and performance of the screeners they employ.

FAA believes these efforts will improve the quality of the personnel hired for screening positions, provide them with better training, and give the screening companies greater incentive to retain their best screeners longer in order to meet FAA's new performance standards for certification. Most of these efforts, however, are behind schedule. For example, FAA is 2 years behind schedule in issuing its regulation requiring the certification of screening companies.

FAA has established annual goals, as required by the Government Performance and Results Act, for improving screeners' detection of test objects. However, the agency has lacked an integrated plan that (1) details how its efforts to improve screeners' performance are related to achieving its goals, (2) identifies and prioritizes problems with screeners' performance that require resolving, and (3) provides budget and milestone information for addressing these problems. FAA has been developing such an integrated management plan to guide its checkpoint screening improvement efforts, but although elements of the plan are being implemented, it is not complete. Furthermore, FAA's method for calculating the achievement of one goal—the detection of dangerous objects in carry-on bags—does not produce meaningful results. It combined the results of two separate types of tests—for detecting standard test objects and for detecting improvised explosive devices—both of which were performed in fiscal year 1998 and again in fiscal year 1999. But during 1999, FAA increased the number of tests using the more easily detected standard objects and decreased the number of tests using the more difficult-to-detect explosive devices. Consequently, FAA showed progress toward achieving its goal when, in fact, no progress had occurred.

Other Countries' Preboard Screening Practices, Turnover, and Performance

GAO examined preboard passenger screening practices in Belgium, Canada, France, the Netherlands, and the United Kingdom—five countries recommended by FAA and industry representatives. GAO found four areas where screening operations differ from those in the United States: the screeners' qualifications; the screeners' pay and benefits; the institutional responsibility for screening; and the stringency of checkpoint screening procedures.

- Most of the countries require that potential screeners undergo lengthier training, be either citizens or long-term residents, and be individually certified for screening work.
- In most of the countries, screeners receive higher salaries and more benefits than do screeners in this country. For example, screeners in

Belgium receive wages equivalent to about $14 per hour, and screeners in the Netherlands receive what they regard as "middle income" wages. In most countries, the screeners also receive health and/or vacation benefits.

- The responsibility for screening rests with either the government or the airport, not with air carriers, as it does in the United States. Although security companies are commonly hired to staff screening checkpoints, the companies report directly to the government or the airport authority.

- Some nations direct screeners to "pat down" passengers after metal detectors go off or at random to increase the screeners' effectiveness. All five countries allow only ticketed passengers to pass through the checkpoint, allowing the screeners to be more attentive to a smaller number of people. Several countries also have a more visible police presence near their checkpoints.

In addition, turnover for screeners is lower in all five countries than in the United States. Among these countries, the highest reported turnover rate was about 50 percent a year, and one country had an annual turnover rate of less than 5 percent. Furthermore, although the countries did not make data on the performance of their screeners available to GAO, the performance of screeners in at least one country was better than in the United States. Joint testing by FAA and this country, using consistent procedures and test objects, demonstrated that the other country's screeners were able to detect the objects at better than twice the rate of U.S. screeners.[2] However, without specific performance data, GAO could not determine whether any of the differences found in the other countries improve screeners' performance in those countries or would improve screeners' performance in the United States.

Recommendations

So that FAA can better implement its efforts to improve screeners' performance, GAO recommends that the Secretary of Transportation direct the Administrator of FAA to do the following:

- Require that FAA's integrated checkpoint screening management plan be promptly completed, implemented, continuously monitored and updated, and periodically evaluated for effectiveness.

---

[2]The results of these tests and the identity of the participant country are sensitive security information and cannot be released publicly.

- For reporting under the Government Performance and Results Act, establish separate goals for the detection of standard test objects and improvised explosive devices concealed in carry-on baggage.

Agency Comments

GAO provided the Department of Transportation with a draft of this report for review and comment. GAO met with officials from FAA, including the Associate Administrator for Civil Aviation Security, who were responding for the Department of Transportation. These officials generally agreed with the facts presented in the draft report and provided technical clarifications, which were incorporated as appropriate.

FAA officials agreed that the performance of checkpoint screeners needs to improve and that the agency's integrated checkpoint screening management plan is not complete. FAA officials agreed with the draft report's recommendation to promptly complete the plan but added that other than the program cost data, it is essentially complete. FAA expects to complete the cost data by the end of 2000. FAA, however, did not concur with the draft report's recommendation that, for reporting under the Government Performance and Results Act, it establish separate goals for the detection of standard test objects and improvised explosive devices concealed in carry-on baggage. FAA commented that, although it agreed with the intent of the recommendation, it nevertheless believes that it is reasonable to aggregate the test results for use in assessing the agency's performance under the Government Performance and Results Act, since the Department of Transportation tries to limit the number of goals established under the act. While GAO agrees that efforts should be made to limit the number of goals, the measurement information required by the Results Act must nevertheless be meaningful and provide the agency with a clear picture of its progress toward meeting its established goals. GAO continues to believe that the progress shown in meeting FAA's current goal is not meaningful—since it can, and does, show improved performance when in fact none exists—and that the goal needs to be revised.

FAA officials were also concerned that the draft report did not provide FAA's perspective on the role cultural and other concerns play in countries' approaches to screening. They noted that what is acceptable to the public elsewhere may not be acceptable in the United States. The officials said that FAA must be aware of the need to protect civil liberties and privacy when considering checkpoint procedures and equipment. The draft report was revised to include their views. Additionally, these officials commented that the numbers of airports and screeners in the countries GAO visited are significantly lower than in the United States, but they provided no information on how these facts affect screeners' performance, turnover, and human factors concerns.

Chapter 1

Introduction

Although more than a decade has passed since the last bombing of a U.S. airliner—the 1988 explosion on Pan Am Flight 103 over Lockerbie, Scotland, that killed 270 people—U.S. aircraft are still believed to be a target for terrorist attacks. According to the Federal Bureau of Investigation, trends in terrorism point toward large-scale incidents designed for maximum destruction, terror, and media impact—exactly the effect of attacks on aviation. Recent events show that concern about such attacks is not unfounded. Philippine police uncovered a plot in 1995 to blow up as many as 12 U.S. airliners in the Pacific region on a single day. Equally ominous is the fact that terrorist activities are posing a threat domestically. For example, a suspected terrorist was apprehended in December 1999 while attempting to enter the country with bomb components, including some small enough to be brought onto an aircraft. The knowledge and materials to build explosive devices that are difficult to detect are readily available and, as a result, the potential for the destruction of aircraft and great loss of life has increased.

Because of this threat to commercial aviation, the Federal Aviation Administration (FAA), which is responsible for the safety and security of civil aviation in the United States, requires various security measures be in place at the nation's airports. Over the past 25 years, FAA has directed that air carriers and airports control access to airport buildings, facilities, and aircraft; question passengers to better ensure that their baggage and its contents have been solely under the passengers' control; scan the checked baggage of certain passengers; and in some cases, match the checked baggage onboard aircraft with enplaning passengers. Of the various security measures, one of the most crucial is the screening of passengers and their carry-on baggage before the passengers board their flights.

Screening Passengers Is a Key Line of Defense

In 1973, to counteract the then-growing number of aircraft hijackings, FAA directed that all passengers be screened, along with their carry-on baggage, before they board an aircraft. Since that time, all passengers have been screened at airport checkpoints, and today, screening personnel—termed screeners—check over 2 million individuals and their bags each day for weapons, explosives, and other dangerous articles that could pose a threat to the safety of an aircraft and those aboard it.

Screeners are a key line of defense against the introduction of dangerous items into the aviation system. All passengers and anyone else who seeks to enter secure areas at the nation's airports must pass through screening checkpoints and be cleared by screeners. At all commercial airports in the United States, screeners

- examine carry-on baggage with X-ray machines to locate any dangerous objects,
- scan passengers with metal detectors to identify any hidden metallic objects, and
- conduct physical searches of items, including those that cannot be scanned by X-ray machines—such as baby carriers or lead-shielded containers—or bags that have been X-rayed and contain unidentifiable objects that could be a threat.

In addition to the routine checkpoint process used for screening every passenger, screeners select carry-on bags at random and search them or use explosive detection equipment to determine if traces of explosives are present on the baggage.[1] After passing through a checkpoint, a person can move about freely in the airport's public secured areas. Figure 1 shows screeners operating a typical checkpoint.

---

[1]FAA had deployed this equipment, referred to as explosive trace detectors, to 84 domestic airports as of April 2000, and it plans deployments to additional airports.

Figure 1: Screeners Operating a Typical Security Checkpoint at an Airport

Source: FAA.

Each year, the nation's screeners detect thousands of dangerous objects that individuals intentionally or inadvertently attempt to carry though checkpoints. From 1990 through 1999, screeners located nearly 23,000 firearms and numerous explosive devices, resulting in over 9,400 arrests. Table 1 shows the number of firearms and explosive devices detected each year.

Table 1: Number of Firearms and Explosive Devices Detected by Airport Screeners, Calendar Years 1990-99

Year	Number of firearms detected	Number of explosive devices detected[a]
1990	2,853	15
1991	1,919	94
1992	2,608	167
1993	2,798	251
1994	2,994	505
1995	2,390	631
1996	2,155	353
1997	2,067	2,764
1998	1,515	[b]
1999	1,570	[b]
Total	**22,869**	**4,780**

[a]FAA believes that the data for explosive devices may be misleading because these items have not been consistently reported. The 1997 data are particularly unreliable because they include mace or pepper spray canisters, fireworks, flares, and other items that, while dangerous on an aircraft, would not likely be used to hjack or damage an airplane. Because of the inconsistencies and irregularities in the data reported by airports, FAA no longer reports these data.

[b]Not available.

Source: FAA.

Screeners do not have police powers and cannot make arrests when they discover dangerous objects. At larger airports, officers are generally stationed on the premises and, when summoned to a screening checkpoint, make arrests as warranted. Smaller airports may not have law enforcement officers present, but FAA's regulations require that law enforcement personnel be available to respond to any incidents.

Passenger Screening Is a Shared Responsibility

The responsibility for screening passengers and carry-on baggage is shared by FAA and air carriers. FAA's regulations requiring the screening of passengers are contained in 14 C.F.R. part 108 and provide basic standards for the equipment and procedures to be used. Additionally, the regulations require each air carrier to have an FAA-approved security program that provides detailed requirements and procedures for screening passengers and their property. All U.S. carriers have adopted the Air Carrier Standard Security Program that FAA developed in consultation with the airline industry. Consequently, all carriers follow similar security procedures.

Furthermore, FAA's regulations establish minimum employment and training standards for screeners. Among other things, these standards specify that screeners possess basic aptitudes and physical abilities, including color perception, visual and aural acuity, physical coordination, and motor skills; know how to read, write, and speak English; and complete 12 hours of classroom training and 40 hours of on-the-job training. Screeners do not need to be U.S. citizens or resident aliens, but if they are not, they must have an authorization from the U.S. Immigration and Naturalization Service to work in the United States. Screeners are required to have completed high school, have an equivalency degree, or have an adequate combination of education and experience.

Air carriers are responsible for conducting screening operations that meet FAA's requirements. An air carrier can use its own employees to screen passengers or contract with another air carrier or a security company to do the screening in accordance with the air carrier's security program. Some air carriers use their own employees to operate screening checkpoints. Most, however, hire independent security firms to do the screening. Currently, almost 100 security companies, employing an estimated 18,000 screeners, are operating at U.S. airports. At large airports, several different screening companies usually operate checkpoints under contract with various airlines. The air carriers are required by FAA to maintain oversight of the checkpoint operations and ensure that all of FAA's requirements are met.

FAA is responsible for overseeing and monitoring the effectiveness of passenger screening and for enforcing compliance with its regulations. As part of this responsibility, FAA inspects the operation of the checkpoints and conducts tests of screeners' ability to detect dangerous objects—called compliance tests. FAA special agents pose as passengers and attempt to get weapons and other dangerous objects though checkpoints by concealing the items either in carry-on baggage or on their own bodies. FAA conducts these tests without notice, using a standard set of test objects, such as guns, or other objects called improvised explosive devices, that are more difficult to detect.[2] Any time a screener fails to detect a standard test object or follow the approved procedures during its tests, FAA can issue a violation to the air carrier responsible for the checkpoint and assess a fine of up to $11,000. FAA regards improvised explosive devices as a tool for training screeners to detect devices that mimic those used by terrorists and does not impose any fines if screeners fail to detect them.

Concerns Over the Effectiveness of Passenger Screening Are Long-Standing

Concerns have long existed over screeners' ability to detect weapons and other dangerous objects. In 1978, FAA's tests indicated that 13 percent of the test objects concealed in carry-on bags passed through X-ray examination without being detected—a rate that was considered "significant and alarming" by both FAA and the airline industry at that time. An FAA-industry task force in 1979 attributed this level of missed objects to personnel factors such as high employee turnover, low pay, and inadequate training. In two 1987 reports, we pointed out that about 20 percent of test objects were still not being identified during the screening process, in large part because of the same personnel factors—turnover, pay, and training.[3]

According to additional studies conducted in the mid- to late 1990s by FAA, the National Research Council, and university researchers, it is evident that there is room for substantial improvement in airport screening. These studies continued to point out concerns about screeners' pay, turnover, and training and the impact of these factors on screeners' performance.

[2]Improvised explosive devices consist of simulated explosives and various modular, off-the-shelf components.

[3]*Aviation Security: FAA Preboard Passenger Screening Test Results* (GAO/RCED-87-125FS, Apr. 30, 1987) and *Aviation Security: FAA Needs Preboard Passenger Screening Performance Standards* (GAO/RCED-87-182, July 24, 1987).

Moreover, some of these studies indicated that screeners' poor performance was a principal weakness of the passenger screening system.

The Congress recognized the problems with screeners' performance and passed legislation in the 1990s to improve screening. Following the bombing of Pan Am Flight 103, the Congress passed the Aviation Security Improvement Act of 1990 to increase the effectiveness of the nation's aviation security system. The act mandated programmatic and organizational changes to FAA's security program, including more stringent employment, education, and training standards for screeners and other airport security personnel. Interest in aviation security was renewed in 1996 by the crash of TWA Flight 800. In response, the White House Commission on Aviation Safety and Security was established and in its initial and final reports, identified aviation security as a national issue and made a number of recommendations to improve it. These recommendations included the purchase and deployment of new screening technologies and equipment and the development of uniform performance standards for the training and testing of screeners and the certification of screening companies. The Congress also enacted two other laws—the Federal Aviation Reauthorization Act of 1996 and the Omnibus Consolidated Appropriations Act of 1997—which, among other things, authorized and provided funding for implementing many of the security recommendations contained in the Commission's report.

Despite these efforts, concerns over screeners' ability to detect dangerous objects remain. Each year, instances occur in which passengers pass through checkpoints at one airport and are subsequently found to have loaded guns at screening checkpoints prior to boarding connecting flights at another airport. Furthermore, screeners' performance in detecting dangerous objects during FAA tests is still not adequate. Since 1997, data on FAA's test results have been designated as sensitive security information and cannot be released publicly; consequently, information on screeners' current performance cannot be discussed in this report. Nevertheless, FAA has acknowledged that screeners' detection of dangerous objects during its testing is unsatisfactory and needs improvement.

Objectives, Scope, and Methodology

Because of the long-standing problems with screeners' performance and congressional interest in effecting lasting improvements in this performance, the Chairman and Ranking Minority Member of the Senate Committee on Commerce, Science, and Transportation and the Chairman and Ranking Minority Member of its Subcommittee on Aviation requested that we review the performance of screening personnel and the efforts being made to improve their performance. We specifically agreed to address the following key questions:

- Since 1990, how accurately have screeners been detecting test objects?
- What are the causes of screeners' performance problems and what efforts is FAA making to address them?
- How do selected foreign countries handle screening operations and do they use practices that could help improve screeners' performance in the United States?

The first question involves sensitive security information that cannot be released publicly. Accordingly, our response was published in a separate limited-distribution report.[4] Our response to the two remaining questions appear in this report.

To obtain an overall perspective on screeners' performance, we reviewed relevant literature focusing on the causes of performance problems, efforts to increase screeners' proficiency, and approaches to improving checkpoint operations. We also reviewed our past reports on aviation security and reports by the Department of Transportation's Office of Inspector General.

To determine the causes of screeners' performance problems and the status of FAA's initiatives to improve their performance, we obtained and reviewed FAA documents that described screening equipment research, development, and deployment efforts; the relationship of human factors to screeners' problems; and the development and implementation of FAA initiatives, including those establishing (1) criteria for selecting screeners, (2) better testing and training practices, and (3) a program for certifying screening companies. We also reviewed FAA's goals for improving screeners' performance and discussed the rationale for these goals and the plans for measuring progress in achieving them with cognizant FAA officials. We also met with FAA officials in Washington, D.C., and at FAA's Technical Center in Atlantic City, New Jersey, to obtain information on the efforts being undertaken to identify causes of performance problems and to implement solutions.

---

[4]*Aviation Security: Screeners Continue to Have Difficulty Detecting Dangerous Objects* (GAO/RCED-00-159, June 2000).

Additionally, we met with representatives of five air carriers, seven security companies, two screening equipment manufacturers, and two aviation industry associations to obtain their perspectives on the performance of screeners and the actions being taken to improve performance. We visited five large airports—Hartsfield Atlanta International Airport; Dallas/Fort Worth International Airport; Los Angeles International Airport; John F. Kennedy International Airport; and Seattle/Tacoma International Airport—to meet with screeners and to discuss screening with air carrier and security company officials. At each location, we also met with local FAA field office staff and the airport's FAA Federal Security Manager.

To determine how screening operations are handled in other countries, we visited Belgium, Canada, France, the Netherlands, and the United Kingdom. We selected these countries for a variety of reasons, such as recommendations of FAA and aviation industry officials, the active role these countries have in international aviation security organizations, and the generally high level of concern for aviation security in these countries. In each country we visited, we met with government and airport officials to discuss the overall institutional framework for passenger screening; the procedures for conducting screening; the requirements for training and certifying screeners; and the compensation, benefits, and career opportunities provided to screeners. We toured major airports in each of these countries and observed screening checkpoints in operation. In Canada and the Netherlands, we also met with screeners to learn about the positive and negative aspects of their jobs. Because of the sensitive nature of security information, we were unable to obtain data on screeners' performance from these countries.

We conducted our work from April 1999 through June 2000 in accordance with generally accepted government auditing standards.

Chapter 2

Long-Standing Problems and Program Delays Hinder Improvements in Screeners' Performance

No single problem causes checkpoint screeners to fail to detect dangerous objects in carry-on bags or on passengers' bodies. Several long-standing and long-recognized problems combine to reduce the screeners' effectiveness, most notably

- the rapid turnover among screeners that leaves few experienced personnel at the checkpoints and
- inattention to "human factors" issues, such as the repetitive tasks and stress involved in the work, individuals' aptitudes for the work, and the need for adequate training in spotting concealed objects that may be dangerous.

FAA has several interrelated initiatives under way to improve checkpoint screeners' performance, including improvements in procedures for selecting and training screeners, better monitoring and testing of screeners, and a certification program for screening companies. Although the initiatives hold promise, they have not been fully implemented and are behind schedule. Furthermore, FAA has established goals for improving screeners' performance, but it (1) has yet to complete an integrated management plan to tie its initiatives to achieving its goals and (2) has not adequately measured its progress in achieving one of its goals.

Rapid Turnover and Human Factors Problems Reduce Screeners' Effectiveness

Because the screening equipment at airport checkpoints does not automatically detect dangerous objects, the effectiveness of the screeners operating the equipment is vital to maintaining the security of the aviation system. It is the screeners who must determine whether an image on an X-ray screen or the triggering of a metal detector's alarm indicates a security concern and, if so, what action should be taken to resolve the concern. FAA, the aviation industry, and others have long recognized that checkpoint screeners are not more successful in their detection of dangerous objects for several reasons. Two of the primary reasons are the rapid turnover among screeners and human factors issues.

The rapid turnover among screeners has been a long-standing problem that affects performance. Turnover was cited as a concern in studies as early as 1979. The studies have found that the high turnover rate means that checkpoints are rarely staffed by screeners with much experience. For instance, one study found that about 90 percent of all screeners at any given checkpoint had less than 6 months' experience.[1] At one airport we visited, we found that, during a 3-month period in 1999, 114 of the 167 screeners (68 percent) hired had quit their jobs. Furthermore, of the 993 screeners trained at this airport over about a 1-year period, only 142 (14 percent) were still employed at the end of that year.

Not only has turnover been an historical problem, but it is worse today than it was in the past. In 1987, we reported that turnover among screeners at some airports was about 100 percent in a 12-month period;[2] by 1994, FAA was reporting that the turnover at some airports was 100 percent in a 10-month period.[3] For the 12 months from May 1998 through April 1999, turnover averaged 126 percent among screeners at 19 large airports, according to data the airports reported to FAA. Five of the airports reported turnover of 200 percent or more, with one reporting turnover of 416 percent. Table 2 lists the turnover rates for screeners at 19 large airports during this period.

Table 2: Turnover Rates for Screeners at 19 Large airports, May 1998-April 1999

City (airport)	Annual turnover rate (percentage)
Atlanta (Hartsfield Atlanta International)	375
Baltimore (Baltimore-Washington International)	155
Boston (Logan International)	207
Chicago (Chicago-O'Hare International)	200

[1]*Development of Decision-Centered Interventions for Airport Security Checkpoints* (DOT/FAA/CT-94/27, Aug. 1994); *Review of the Literature Related to Screening Airline Passenger Baggage* (DOT/FAA/CT/94/108, Oct. 1994).

[2]*Aviation Security: FAA Needs Preboard Passenger Screening Performance Standards* (GAO/RCED-87-182, July 24, 1987).

[3]DOT/FAA/CT94/108.

(Continued From Previous Page)

City (airport)	Annual turnover rate (percentage)
Dallas-Ft. Worth (Dallas/Ft. Worth International)	156
Denver (Denver International)	193
Detroit (Detroit Metro Wayne County)	79
Honolulu (Honolulu International)	37
Houston (Houston Intercontinental)	237
Los Angeles (Los Angeles International)	88
Miami (Miami International)	64
New York (John F. Kennedy International)	53
Orlando (Orlando International)	100
San Francisco (San Francisco International)	110
San Juan (Luis Munoz Marin International)	70
Seattle (Seattle-Tacoma International)	140
St. Louis (Lambert St. Louis International)	416
Washington (Washington-Dulles International)	90
Washington (Ronald Reagan Washington National)	47
Average turnover	**126**

Source: FAA.

Both FAA and the aviation industry attribute the high turnover to the low wages screeners receive, the minimal benefits, and the daily stress of the job. Generally, screeners get paid at or near the minimum wage. We found that some of the screening companies at many of the nation's largest airports paid screeners a starting salary of $6 an hour or less, and at some airports, the starting salary was the minimum wage—$5.15 an hour. It is common for the starting wages at airport fast-food restaurants to be higher than the wages screeners receive. For instance, at one airport we visited, the screeners' wages started as low as $6.25 an hour, whereas the starting wage at one of the airport's fast-food restaurants was $7 an hour.

"Human factors" refers to the demands a job places on the capabilities of, and the constraints it imposes on, the people doing it. For screeners, the human factors issues cited in past studies include the repetitive tasks screeners perform, the close and constant monitoring required to spot the rare appearances of dangerous objects, and the stress involved in dealing with the public, who may dislike being screened or demand faster action to avoid missing their flights.[4] FAA's research has found that too little attention has been paid to (1) individuals' aptitudes for effectively performing screening duties, (2) the sufficiency of the training provided to screeners and how well they comprehended it, and (3) the monotony of the job and the distractions that reduce screeners' vigilance.

As a result, according to FAA research officials, screeners are placed on the job who do not have the necessary knowledge, skills, or abilities to perform the work effectively and who then find the duties tedious and unstimulating. The President's Commission on Aviation Security and Terrorism and the White House Commission on Aviation Safety and Security both concluded that better selection, training, and testing of screeners could improve their performance. The 1999 National Research Council's report assessing explosive detection equipment also found that FAA needed to improve the training, testing, and qualification procedures for the screeners operating the equipment.

Initiatives to Improve Screeners' Performance Under Way, but Key Aspects Are Behind Schedule

FAA has undertaken several separate initiatives that are designed to address the rapid turnover and human factors problems affecting screeners and thus improve their performance. These initiatives include

- improving the hiring and preparation of screeners through selection tests, computer-based training, and competency tests;
- a system to keep screeners alert and monitor their performance by periodically projecting images of dangerous objects onto the monitors of the X-ray machines at checkpoints and recording the screeners' responses; and

---

[4]Reports on the human factors involved in checkpoint screening go back 20 years; among the most recent are those of the President's Commission on Aviation Security and Terrorism, 1990; the White House Commission on Aviation Safety and Security, 1997; and the National Academy of Sciences *Assessment of Technologies Deployed to Improve Aviation Security*, 1999.

- a certification program to make screening companies, along with the air carriers, accountable for the training and performance of the screeners they employ.

Table 3 summarizes these initiatives and the improvements FAA expects to result. FAA is making progress with these initiatives, although delays have occurred.

Table 3: FAA's Initiatives to Improve Screeners' Performance

FAA initiative	Select candidate with screener potential	Ensure screener is trained and ready to perform	Ensure screener is alert and monitored	Increase pay, and reduce turnover
		Expected improvement		
Hiring and preparation of screeners:				
Selection testing	X			X
Computer-based training		X		
Competency testing		X		
Threat image projection system		X	X	
Certification of screening companies		X	X	X

Improving the Hiring and Preparation of Screeners

Through separate initiatives, FAA is attempting to improve the selection of candidates for screening positions, improve their training, and ensure their readiness to perform their duties. First, FAA is developing standardized selection tests to help screening companies identify applicants who have natural aptitudes for checkpoint screening tasks. FAA's research has shown that new screeners who lack certain aptitudes are more likely to quit and that an effective selection process could result in improved performance, maximum benefit from training resources, greater job satisfaction, and reduced turnover. The selection tests will assess applicants' spatial memory and visual perception, among other things. After validating one or more selection tests, FAA will offer them to air carriers and screening companies for their use. According to FAA officials, these tests should be helpful to screening companies, and although they will not be required, FAA officials are hopeful that screening companies will adopt and use them.

Second, to improve the quality and consistency of screeners' training, FAA has been deploying computer-based training systems at the nation's airports. These systems instruct trainees in all aspects of checkpoint screening, including how to interpret X-ray images of carry-on baggage and how to screen passengers. FAA believes computer-based training has advantages because (1) screeners can learn at their own pace and have better opportunities to develop detection skills, (2) training is more consistent, and (3) overall training time can be reduced. An FAA study determined that screeners who had computer-based training detected dangerous objects more accurately than screeners who had traditional classroom instruction.

FAA is behind schedule in deploying the training systems, however, and those in place are not being fully used. As of March 2000, FAA had the systems in place at only 36 of the 79 airports it had expected to equip by the end of the previous fiscal year. The agency attributes the delay to funding problems and to a decision to replace 30 of the deployed systems with a different computer system preferred by the airlines. FAA plans to deploy systems to another 31 airports by the end of fiscal year 2001. Meanwhile, the systems already deployed are not being fully used at some airports because the equipment is located in one screening company's area and other screening companies do not want to send their personnel to a competitor's area. We reported on this situation in April 1998,[5] and it continues to exist. An FAA official whose office is responsible for deploying equipment said that the agency plans, where possible, to deploy future systems to multiple locations within airports to minimize this problem.

Third, FAA is developing three tests to measure screeners' mastery of critical job elements. Screeners will be required to take (1) a readiness test after their initial training and before they begin on-the-job training, (2) a training test after they complete 40 hours of on-the-job training, and (3) a review test after they complete required recurrent training. These tests will help ensure that screeners have the knowledge and skills to perform their jobs effectively and can perform at a prescribed level. FAA expects the tests, which will be computer-based, will impose more control and consistency in training. The agency is developing specific requirements and guidelines for the tests, but it will not require them until it begins certifying

---

[5]*Aviation Security: Implementation of Recommendations Is Under Way, but Completion Will Take Several Years* (GAO/RCED-98-102, Apr. 24, 1998).

screening companies in 2002. Thus, it will be several years before any benefits can be expected from these tests.

Keeping Screeners Alert and Monitoring Their Performance

Because screeners check thousands of passengers and their baggage yet rarely see dangerous objects being brought through airport checkpoints, remaining vigilant is difficult. To help screeners remain alert, train them to become more adept at detecting harder-to-spot objects such as improvised explosive devices, and continuously measure their performance, FAA is deploying a threat image projection system. This automated system is an enhancement to the X-ray machines used at checkpoints. As checkpoint personnel routinely scan passengers' carry-on bags, the system occasionally projects images of dangerous objects, including guns and explosives, on the X-ray machines' screens. Screeners are expected to identify the generated images as dangerous objects. The system records the screeners' responses to the projected images, providing a measure of their performance while keeping them more alert. By frequently exposing screeners to a variety of images of dangerous objects on the X-ray screens, the system provides continuous on-the-job training.

Furthermore, the threat image projection system and analyses of its data are critical to a number of FAA's efforts to improve screeners' performance. The data will be used to analyze performance—by individual screener, screening company, airport, air carrier, or dangerous object—to determine areas of weakness. The data will also be used to assess and validate the results of FAA's efforts to improve screeners' performance, such as by allowing the agency to compare the results of screener selection tests or computer-based training with on-the-job performance. The data from the system can also be used to tailor recurrent training to meet individual screeners' needs. In addition, the system's data are critical to FAA's efforts to establish the performance standards that screening companies will be expected to meet in order to be certified.

Deployment of the threat image projection system, however, is behind schedule. FAA had planned to begin installing 284 units on existing X-ray machines at 19 large airports in April 1998, but because of hardware and software problems, FAA changed its plans and decided to purchase new X-ray machines already equipped with the threat image projection system. As of March 2000, FAA had deployed 30 of these machines at six large airports for testing, and beginning in mid-2000, it will begin purchasing and deploying another 1,380 such machines. FAA expects to have the system in place at the largest airports by the end of fiscal year 2001 and at all airports by the end of fiscal 2003. Unfortunately, these delays in the system's deployment have already impeded another key initiative to improve screeners' performance—the certification of screening companies.

Certifying Screening Companies

In response to a mandate in the Federal Aviation Reauthorization Act of 1996 and a recommendation from the 1997 report of the White House Commission on Aviation Safety and Security, FAA is creating a program to certify the companies that staff screening checkpoints. As currently proposed, the certification program will establish performance standards—an action we recommended in 1987[6]—that the screening companies will have to meet to earn and retain certification; require that all screeners pass computer-based tests after initial, on-the-job, and recurrent training; and require that all air carriers have the threat image projection system on the X-ray machines at their checkpoints so that screeners' performance can be measured to ensure that FAA's standards are met. FAA believes that the need to meet certification standards will give the screening companies a greater incentive to raise screeners' wages and improve training in order to obtain better screeners and keep them longer. Most of the air carrier, screening company, and airport representatives we contacted said they believe certification has the potential to improve screeners' performance.

FAA plans to issue a regulation establishing the certification program by May 2001, over 4½ years after the passage of the Reauthorization Act and more than 2 years later than its earlier estimated issuance date of March 1999. Moreover, before FAA can begin certifying screening companies, it must (1) complete the installation of the threat image projection system needed to set standards and measure screeners' performance, (2) review and approve the screening companies' security programs, and (3) establish a staff to handle the certification program. Because the threat image projection system will not be completely installed before the end of fiscal year 2003, FAA is exploring other ways to set standards and is considering using the results from its compliance tests in conjunction with available data from the threat image projection system. According to FAA, the first certifications of screening companies will not take place until 2002.

---

[6]GAO/RCED-87-182, July 24, 1987.

More Effective Use of Management Tools Can Help Improve Screeners' Performance

The Government Performance and Results Act (Results Act) requires each federal agency to set multiyear strategic goals and strategies for reaching them, as well as measure performance toward achieving the goals. The measurement information is to give the agency and others a clear picture of its progress toward meeting the established goals. In accordance with this requirement, FAA included in its 1998 strategic plan goals for measuring its progress in improving screeners' performance.[7] Using the results of its screener compliance tests as a performance measure, the agency established goals for increasing the detection of dangerous objects carried by FAA agents in carry-on baggage and on the body through metal detectors.

In addition to establishing goals, FAA began in early 1999 to develop an integrated checkpoint screening management plan to help it meet its improvement goals and better focus its efforts to improve screeners' performance. According to FAA officials, the plan will (1) incorporate FAA's screener improvement goals and detail how its efforts relate to the goals' achievement; (2) identify and prioritize checkpoint and human factors problems that need to be resolved; and (3) provide measures for addressing the performance problems, including related milestone and budget information. Such a plan is needed to provide management with the information it needs to guide its various planning, research and development, and equipment deployment efforts; integrate those efforts toward common achievable goals; and prioritize funding needs. An integrated plan is also essential to help FAA track the status of its various initiatives to improve screeners' performance and to take actions to help keep the agency on schedule.

However, the plan has yet to be completed. During our review, FAA security officials told us several times that the plan would be completed shortly, and they provided various completion dates, but the completion dates were not met. FAA officials told us that elements of the plan are nevertheless being implemented. For example, FAA consolidated the responsibility for screening checkpoint improvements under a single program manager responsible for overseeing the development of the plan and for coordinating screener improvement efforts at FAA headquarters,

---

[7]FAA views specific data relating to these goals, as well as other information relating to screeners' detection rates, to be sensitive security information that cannot be publicly released.

FAA field locations, and the agency's Technical Center in Atlantic City, New Jersey. In addition, quarterly briefings are provided to the Associate Administrator for Civil Aviation Security on the status of the initiatives covered in the plan. Nevertheless, these officials stated that cost data for the plan must still be developed and they do not expect these data until the end of the year.

FAA acknowledges that it did not approach its Results Act goal for improving the detection of dangerous objects carried on the body through metal detectors. It did, however, report almost meeting its goal for improving the detection of dangerous objects in carry-on baggage. Nevertheless, our analysis shows that FAA did not use a methodology that provides a consistent measure of progress toward this goal. Although FAA measured screeners' detection rates for both standard test objects and explosive devices in carry-on baggage for both fiscal year 1998 and fiscal year 1999 and then calculated a combined detection rate for each fiscal year, it modified its testing in fiscal year 1999. In that year, FAA conducted proportionally fewer tests using the harder-to-spot improvised explosive devices and more tests using the more readily spotted standard test objects than it conducted the year before. As a result, the combined detection rate for fiscal year 1999 was higher than for fiscal year 1998, even though the detection rates for improvised explosive devices and for standard test objects each declined during fiscal year 1999. Had FAA conducted both tests in the same proportions during both fiscal years, the detection rate for fiscal 1999 would have been lower than it was for fiscal year 1998.

FAA security officials said that the choice of objects used during compliance testing is up to the agents conducting the tests. They also said security officials had not been aware that proportionally fewer tests would be done with improvised explosive devices and they had not considered the impact of this difference. They also said that, when they established the goals, the agency anticipated a wider deployment of some screener improvement initiatives, such as the threat image projection and computer-based training systems. Consequently, FAA officials said they will likely revise the goals to reflect the improvements in screeners' performance that they now believe can be attained during the next 3 years. They do not plan to revise the methodology that aggregates the test results for carry-on baggage.

Conclusions

Despite concerns about checkpoint screeners' ability to detect and prevent weapons and explosives from being taken aboard aircraft, long-standing—

and long-recognized—problems affecting screeners' performance, such as rapid turnover and inadequate attention to human factors, remain. FAA's initiatives to address these problems may, in the long run, help considerably; however, the continuing delays in implementing the agency's two key initiatives—the threat image projection system and the screening company certification program—are prolonging the time before the public can have greater assurance that dangerous objects are prevented from being brought aboard aircraft.

We are encouraged that FAA is taking actions to improve the management of its screener initiatives. These actions—adopting performance goals to measure its progress, developing and implementing an integrated plan to better focus and manage its checkpoint screening improvement initiatives, and consolidating these initiatives under a single program manager—will be crucial to guiding the implementation of FAA's initiatives. However, FAA has operated far too long without a complete integrated plan, and its method for calculating progress toward improving detection rates does not produce meaningful results that present a clear picture of progress. Finalizing the integrated plan would provide a document that FAA management could use to track the agency's progress in implementing efforts to improve screeners' performance. Establishing separate goals for the detection of standard test objects and improvised explosive devices in carry-on baggage would provide a more meaningful measure of FAA's progress toward improving screeners' performance.

Recommendations

To better implement FAA's efforts to improve screeners' performance and to provide a valid basis for evaluating FAA's progress in achieving its performance goals for screeners, we recommend that the Secretary of Transportation direct the Administrator, FAA, to take the following actions:

- Require that FAA's integrated checkpoint screening management plan, which ties together the various initiatives for improving screeners' performance, be promptly completed, implemented, continuously monitored and updated, and evaluated for effectiveness.
- For reporting under the Government Performance and Results Act, establish separate goals for the detection of standard test objects and improvised explosive devices concealed in carry-on baggage.

Agency Comments and Our Evaluation

FAA officials generally concurred with the facts presented in our draft report and agreed that the performance of checkpoint screeners needs to improve. FAA officials also agreed with our recommendation to promptly complete the agency's integrated checkpoint screening management plan. FAA pointed out that the plan is now essentially complete except for cost data, and that these data are expected to be completed by the end of 2000. However, they added that the plan is an iterative working document that changes as projects and activities are added or finished, and in that sense the plan, when completed, will never be finalized. FAA officials stated that the latest iteration of the plan is reviewed and approved quarterly at program meetings with the Associate Administrator for Civil Aviation Security.

FAA, however, did not concur with the draft report's recommendation that, for reporting under the Government Performance and Results Act, it establish separate goals for the detection of standard test objects and improvised explosive devices concealed in carry-on baggage. FAA commented that, although it agreed with the intent of the recommendation, it nevertheless believes that it is reasonable to aggregate the test results for assessments under the Results Act, since the Department of Transportation, as the reporting agency, tries to limit the number of goals established under the act. While GAO agrees that efforts should be made to limit the number of goals, measurement information required by the Results Act must nevertheless be meaningful and provide the agency with a clear picture of its progress toward meeting its established goals. GAO continues to believe that the progress shown in meeting FAA's current goal is not meaningful—since it can, and does, show improved performance when in fact none exists—and that the goal needs to be revised.

Chapter 3

Selected Foreign Countries' Screening Practices, Turnover, and Performance

Aviation security is a problem that the United States does not face alone; it is a worldwide concern. In fact, far more incidents of aviation terrorism have occurred in other parts of the world than in the United States. For instance, during the one-year period ending December 1999, 13 hijackings of aircraft occurred; none of these incidents took place in the United States or involved a U.S. airline.

Because of their concern about aviation security, most nations have procedures for screening passengers and their bags before allowing them aboard commercial airliners. In visits to five countries, we found that although passengers are screened there much as they are in the United States, some practices and policies differ. For example, in most of these countries we found

- more extensive qualifications and training for screeners,
- higher pay for screeners,
- screening responsibilities assigned to the airport or government, and
- more stringent checkpoint operations, such as routine "pat down" searches of passengers.

We also found that turnover is not as significant a problem in these other countries as it is in the United States. Furthermore, while data for other countries screeners' performance in detecting dangerous objects were not available, a test conducted jointly by FAA and one of the countries showed that the other country's screeners detected over twice as many test objects as did U.S. screeners. However, there are no other such tests or other performance data available to us and without specific performance data, we could not determine whether any of the differences found in the other countries improve screeners' performance in those countries or would improve screeners' performance in the United States.

Screening Practices in the United States and Five Other Countries Differ

FAA security officials and industry representatives familiar with foreign countries' security operations identified a number of countries that screen passengers effectively. From among these countries, we selected five—Belgium, Canada, France, the Netherlands, and the United Kingdom—to determine if their screening practices differ from those in the United States.

We visited these five countries to observe their screening practices. In general, much of what these countries do to screen passengers is similar to what is done in the United States. All five countries examine the contents of carry-on bags by using X-ray machines or physical searches and scan passengers by using metal detectors. But important differences exist in (1) screeners' qualifications, (2) the pay and benefits screeners receive, (3) the assignment of responsibility for screening, and (4) the operation of screening checkpoints.

Screeners' Qualifications Are More Extensive

Most of the countries we visited had more stringent requirements for hiring and training individuals to become screeners. In the United States, FAA requires that to be hired as a screener, a person must have a high school education or a combination of adequate education and experience; pass a background check; and be able to read, write, and speak English. A screener is not required to be a citizen or to have established residency. Most of the countries we visited had similar education and background check requirements; however, in some countries, a screener must either be a citizen of the country or have resided in the country for a specific length of time. Belgium requires screeners to be citizens and to be fluent in both French and Dutch. The Netherlands requires screeners to have resided in the country for at least 5 years and to be fluent in both Dutch and English. France requires screener candidates to be citizens of a European Union country; because of the close cooperation among police within the European Union, French officials believe this requirement provides assurance that they can obtain adequate background checks. Canada's requirements are similar to those in the United States. Canada requires screeners to be citizens or permanent residents with valid employment authorization documents, and screeners must be able to read, write, and speak either French or English.

The training required to become a screener is more extensive in four of the five countries. FAA requires that screeners in the United States receive 12 hours of classroom training, followed by at least 40 hours of on-the-job training. In contrast, other countries generally require more training. The Netherlands requires candidates for screening positions to train first and become certified as general security officers and then take specialized training to be certified as checkpoint screeners. In the Netherlands, the 40 hours of specialized training for screeners includes classroom work, computer-based training, and role-playing. This is followed by 2 months of on-the-job training and 24 hours of additional training each year for screeners to maintain certification. In Belgium, the basic training for certification as checkpoint screeners includes 40 hours of training on aviation issues. In addition, Belgium requires training in various aviation security topics, such as operating X-ray machines, ranging from 4 to 64 hours. Canada requires 20 hours of classroom training in addition to 40 hours of on-the-job training. After completing the training, Canadian screeners are certified by the government. Once certified, screeners must pass written and practical tests every 2 years to be recertified. In France, screeners must complete 60 hours of training followed by 20 hours of on-the-job training, coupled with tasks such as checking tickets or doing guard duty. These assignments give the screening company opportunities to observe and evaluate new staff and provide additional training if necessary. After completing on-the-job training, new screeners must pass tests administered by the French government.

Pay and Benefits Are Better for Screeners

Another major difference between the United States and most of the other countries we visited is the level of compensation screeners receive. As discussed in chapter 2, screeners in the United States are generally paid at or only slightly above the minimum wage of $5.15 an hour and receive minimal benefits. In the European countries we visited, screeners' pay and benefits are higher. For example, Belgian officials said screeners are paid the equivalent of about $14 to $15 per hour and they receive benefits, such as health care, as required by Belgian law. In the Netherlands, screeners receive a minimum salary, based on a collective labor agreement, that is equivalent to about $7.50 per hour, which Dutch screeners said is at least 25 percent higher than what fast-food restaurants pay and is sufficient to support a middle-income lifestyle. In addition, they receive health care, retirement, and vacation benefits. At one screening company in France screeners earn a starting salary equivalent to about $5.80 per hour with an extra month salary for staying 1 year. In the United Kingdom screeners earn the equivalent of about $8 per hour. Governments in both nations also provide health benefits. In Canada, the starting wage for a screener is the equal to about $5.34 per hour in U.S. funds, more than the starting salary at an airport fast-food restaurant. All Canadian screeners receive health benefits from their provincial governments, and many employers offer additional subsidized health insurance plans. The Canadian government requires that all employers provide paid vacations and paid holidays.

Air Carriers Are Not Responsible for Screening Operations

Most of the five countries we visited do not make air carriers responsible for screening passengers as the United States does and so have more centralized screening operations. At some major U.S. airports, such as John F. Kennedy International and Los Angeles International, airlines may employ four or five different screening companies to operate the checkpoints in their areas of the airport. By contrast, most of the countries we visited assigned the responsibility for screening to the government or to the airport authority, putting one entity in charge of screening for an entire airport. In Belgium, France, and the United Kingdom, the airports are responsible for screening. In Belgium, the airport authority, once a government entity and now private, is responsible for hiring and managing screeners. In France, an airport authority can hire one or more security companies approved by the Ministry of the Interior. The police and customs officials supervise the security companies and their screeners, examining turnover rates and wages, analyzing incident reports, and testing screeners. In the United Kingdom, the airport company itself may contract the screening operations to one or more security companies or choose, as the two largest airports near London have done, to hire screeners directly and manage their work.

In the Netherlands, the government is currently responsible for passenger screening. It employs a security company to conduct the screening operations, and the Dutch Royal Marechaussee—a national police force—oversees the operations. However, the Netherlands is preparing legislation under which the responsibility for implementing checkpoint screening will be transferred to the airport. In Canada, screening responsibility is vested in the air carriers, just as it is in the United States.

According to officials in some of these countries, assigning the responsibility for screening passengers to organizations other than airlines makes a significant difference. They said that air carriers have economic pressures that airports and governments face to a lesser degree. As a result, they said, airports or governments can provide better training and pay better wages than air carriers can. According to officials in the United Kingdom, when an airport hires screeners directly, the screeners can be given a range of security duties beyond staffing the checkpoints and have a greater opportunity for career development. British officials noted that the varied duties and career opportunities improve motivation and performance. Some foreign government and airport officials also pointed out that when several air carriers and security companies are handling screening within one airport, as is the case in the United States, responsibility is fragmented, uniformity is lacking, and competition among the security companies to be the low bidder for the air carriers' screening business puts downward pressure on screeners' wages, making it difficult to attract and retain good screeners.

Checkpoint Operations Are More Stringent

We observed three differences in procedures that made screening more stringent at airports in the countries we visited. First, to help determine if dangerous items are present, screeners in some countries physically search passengers if they set off metal detector alarms. In the United States, screeners use hand-held metal detectors to identify potentially dangerous objects but generally avoid physically touching the passengers. In contrast, screeners in three countries—Belgium, the Netherlands, and the United Kingdom—routinely "pat down" passengers when the alarms on walk-through metal detectors go off. Officials in these countries told us that if an alarm goes off as a passenger walks through a metal detector, screeners are required to physically search the passenger immediately to determine if a dangerous object is present. Officials from these countries said screeners there do not routinely use hand-held metal detectors because, if not used properly, they can fail to detect metal objects. Dutch officials added that a hand-held metal detector can leave the impression that an item such as a belt buckle has caused the alarm, whereas a weapon could be hidden behind the buckle and not be detected by a screener unless touched. Additionally, in the Netherlands and the United Kingdom, screeners will randomly select passengers to be physically searched even though they did not set off alarms. The random searches are conducted because nonmetallic objects can pose a substantial threat to the security of an aircraft; the searches may not only turn up specific items but also deter passengers from attempting to carry these items onto an aircraft.

The second difference in checkpoint operations we observed is that only ticketed passengers are screened and allowed to proceed beyond the checkpoints in all five countries. At most U.S. airports, nonpassengers as well as passengers are allowed though checkpoints and into the secure areas of airports. Officials from some other countries gave a number of reasons for limiting access to checkpoints. Most significant, limiting access to passengers reduces the number of people entering secure areas and consequently reduces the risk that a dangerous object will be brought onto an aircraft. Officials in some countries pointed out that a terrorist could have unticketed accomplices carry components of a bomb through a checkpoint and then assemble the pieces once inside the secure area. These officials also noted that limiting the number of people passing through the checkpoints reduces the burden on screeners, allowing them to be more thorough and minimizing screening costs.

The third difference in how checkpoints are operated is the more visible presence of police and military security personnel. At large airports in the United States, a police presence is required to respond to alerts from checkpoints within 5 minutes. But although uniformed police are stationed in the larger U.S. airport complexes, they are generally not posted at the screening checkpoints. At large airports in the countries we visited, police or military personnel are either at the checkpoints or posted visibly nearby. For example, at Belgium's main airport, police maintain a constant presence in one of two glass-enclosed rooms directly behind the checkpoints. In France and the United Kingdom, armed security forces—often carrying automatic weapons—patrol at or near the checkpoints. In the Netherlands, armed security forces are posted at screening checkpoints for flights that are deemed high risk—a category that includes flights to the United States.

Turnover Is Lower in Five Countries, and Performance May Be Better

Besides the differences in checkpoint operations, other major differences distinguishing screening in the countries we visited and the United States are turnover rates and perhaps performance. While officials were reluctant to give us detailed data on turnover rates for screeners, they did say that the rates were significantly lower there than in the United States. According to officials from these countries, their annual screener turnover rates were about 50 percent or less. The lowest turnover rate was in Belgium, where officials at the country's main airport said that it was less than 4 percent last year. In contrast, turnover rates in the United States averaged 126 percent annually at 19 large airports.

Additionally, screeners in these countries may perform better in detecting dangerous objects. Because of security concerns, foreign country officials would not provide performance data during our visits. Consequently, little information is available to compare the effectiveness of the five countries' screening operations with those in the United States. However, we did find that in 1998, FAA and one of the countries we visited jointly tested screeners' performance using the same objects and procedures at one or more airports in each country. In these tests the detection rate for screeners in the other country was more than twice as high as the rate for screeners in the United States.

FAA has recognized that other countries have different screening practices that may lead to better performance by screeners. In its 1999 proposed rule for the certification of screening companies, FAA noted that experience in other countries seems to indicate that higher compensation and more training may result in lower turnover rates and more effective performance. FAA also noted that the United States can strengthen its screening practices in many areas, several of which—including performance and screeners' work environment—are addressed in its proposed screener certification program. Finally, FAA pointed out that U.S. air carriers and screening companies may want to pursue factors such as more training, higher pay, and more experience to achieve higher performance.

Some Members of Congress have also recognized that the practices of other countries, particularly their training of screeners, may improve screeners' performance. Consequently, legislation was recently proposed to increase screeners' training requirements. Under this proposal (S.2440), introduced in April 2000, screeners would be required to have 40 hours of classroom instruction, plus 40 hours of practical training, before being qualified to provide screening services. As of May 2000, the Senate was still considering this legislation.

At this time, FAA is not considering any changes in U.S. screening practices based on the experiences of other countries. FAA looked at one of the differences we identified—the assignment of responsibility for conducting screening operations—and considered shifting it away from air carriers. However, FAA concluded in a 1999 report to the Congress that there was a lack of consensus in the civil aviation community on any changes in the current system of shared security responsibilities and therefore no change should be made. In other areas, FAA expects to conduct research and examine operational data, both domestically and in conjunction with foreign governments, to determine how various factors affect screeners' performance and retention.

FAA officials noted that some of the screening practices of other countries reflect cultural and other differences between these countries and the United States. In their view, such practices would not be acceptable in this country. They pointed in particular to the routine and frequent patting down of passengers, which they believe the American public would not tolerate. The FAA officials said that protecting an individual's civil liberties and taking into account the American public's low tolerance for what may be perceived as invasions of privacy are high priorities when considering checkpoint procedures and equipment.

Conclusions

Although insufficient information is available to make broad statements on key measures of performance in detecting dangerous objects, other countries may have better approaches to conducting screening activities. The root causes of screeners' problems in this country—frequent turnover and inadequate attention to human factors concerns such as training—do not appear to be as prevalent in some other countries. Furthermore, as indicated in the one instance of joint testing between the United States and another country, the detection of dangerous objects may also be better in other countries. What is not clear, however, is the extent to which each of the different practices identified limits turnover and human factors concerns and improves screeners' performance. Although certain practices, such as higher pay and benefits, can be assumed to reduce turnover and improve job satisfaction, there are no data to determine the impact on turnover and performance of practices such as physical searches of passengers, limitations on access to checkpoints, or the assignment of screening responsibility to airports.

In light of the (1) limited data on the impact of other countries' screening practices on screeners' turnover and performance, (2) FAA's ongoing efforts to improve screeners' performance, and (3) legislation proposed to increase screeners' training requirements, we do not believe it is necessary to add or revise other screening practices at this time. FAA's initiatives, such as the screening company certification program and the implementation of performance standards for screeners, may improve screeners' performance. However, if these initiatives do not bring about satisfactory improvements or if progress is too slow, it may be necessary to consider pursuing some of the strategies and practices other countries use to operate screening checkpoints.

Agency Comments and Our Evaluation

FAA officials said that the draft report did not provide their perspective on the role of cultural and other concerns in countries' screening practices and the public's acceptance of these practices. They noted that what is acceptable to the public elsewhere may not be acceptable in the United States. The officials said that FAA must be aware of the need to protect civil liberties and privacy when considering checkpoint procedures and equipment. We revised the draft report to include their views. They added that there are fewer airports and screeners in these countries than there are in the United States. However, they provided no information on how these factors affect screeners' performance and turnover or on how they influence human factors concerns.

GAO Contacts and Staff Acknowledgments

GAO Contacts

Gerald L. Dillingham, Ph.D. (202) 512-2834

John R. Schulze (202) 512-2834

Staff Acknowledgments

In addition to those named above, Leslie D. Albin, J. Michael Bollinger, A. Donald Cowan, Elizabeth R. Eisenstadt, Curtis L. Groves, David K. Hooper, Barry R. Kime, and Daniel J. Semick made key contributions to this report.

Related GAO Products

Aviation Security: Vulnerabilities Still Exist in the Aviation Security System (GAO/T-RCED-AIMD-00-142, Apr. 6, 2000).

Aviation Security: Slow Progress in Addressing Long-Standing Screener Performance Problems (GAO/T-RCED-00-125, Mar. 16, 2000).

Aviation Security: FAA's Actions to Study Responsibilities and Funding for Airport Security and to Certify Screening Companies (GAO/RCED-99-53, Feb. 25, 1999).

Aviation Security: FAA's Deployments of Equipment to Detect Traces of Explosives (GAO/RCED-99-32R, Nov. 13, 1998).

Aviation Security: Progress Being Made, but Long-Term Attention Is Needed (GAO/T-RCED-98-190, May 14, 1998).

Aviation Security: Implementation of Recommendations Is Underway, but Completion Will Take Several Years (GAO/RCED-98-102, Apr. 24, 1998).

Aviation Security: FAA Needs Preboard Passenger Screening Performance Standards (GAO/RCED-87-182, July 24, 1987).

Aviation Security: FAA Preboard Passenger Screening Test Results (GAO/RCED-87-125FS, Apr. 30, 1987).

Ordering Information

The first copy of each GAO report is free. Additional copies of reports are $2 each. A check or money order should be made out to the Superintendent of Documents. VISA and MasterCard credit cards are accepted, also.

Orders for 100 or more copies to be mailed to a single address are discounted 25 percent.

Orders by mail:
U.S. General Accounting Office
P.O. Box 37050
Washington, DC 20013

Orders by visiting:
Room 1100
700 4th St. NW (corner of 4th and G Sts. NW)
U.S. General Accounting Office
Washington, DC

Orders by phone:
(202) 512-6000
fax: (202) 512-6061
TDD (202) 512-2537

Each day, GAO issues a list of newly available reports and testimony. To receive facsimile copies of the daily list or any list from the past 30 days, please call (202) 512-6000 using a touchtone phone. A recorded menu will provide information on how to obtain these lists.

Orders by Internet:
For information on how to access GAO reports on the Internet, send an e-mail message with "info" in the body to:

info@www.gao.gov

or visit GAO's World Wide Web home page at:

http://www.gao.gov

To Report Fraud, Waste, or Abuse in Federal Programs

Contact one:

- Web site: http://www.gao.gov/fraudnet/fraudnet.htm
- e-mail: fraudnet@gao.gov
- 1-800-424-5454 (automated answering system)

United States
General Accounting Office
Washington, D.C. 20548-0001

Official Business
Penalty for Private Use $300

Address Correction Requested